WEATHER AND SEASONS

By Lynn Cohen

Illustrated by Philip Chalk

Publisher: Roberta Suid
Editor: Mary McClellan
Design and production: Susan Pinkerton

monday morning®

Monday Morning is a registered trademark of
Monday Morning Books, Inc.

Entire contents copyright ©1988 by Monday Morning
Books, Inc., Box 1680, Palo Alto, California 94302

ISBN 0-912107-79-0

Printed in the United States of America
9 8 7 6 5 4 3 2 1

CONTENTS

INTRODUCTION

How many colors are there in a rainbow? Where does rain come from? *Weather and Seasons* offers children four to seven years old the opportunity to explore basic science principles through hands-on experiments and to apply what they learn to the world around them.

Classroom-tested projects encourage children to exercise their sense of wonder as well as their beginning problem-solving and creative thinking abilities. The activities in *Weather and Seasons* guide children to be good observers and to make conclusions based on their observations. Children also develop important thinking skills such as categorizing, comparing, and cause and effect. The activities in the book do not focus exclusively on science. They also integrate the experiments with math, language arts, social living, art, and creative movement activities.

Most of these ideas have been field tested with early childhood students in the East Williston School District in New York, in a nursery school called Kids Korner in Huntington, Long Island, and with the author's own young children, Vicky and Mark. The activities have also been tested in numerous in-service workshops for preschool and primary teachers, who felt these activities were useful and appropriate for this age group.

All children, however, are not the same. They have diversified interests, abilities, and emotions. It is important to consider individual differences when using this book. For the classroom teacher, whole class or small group instruction is recommended. Many activities provide for individual differences in the section "Variations."

Format of the Book

This book is designed for an entire year of weather and seasonal observation. Experiments are grouped according to types of weather—sunny, windy, rainy, and snowy days—so that children can see the relationship of what they are learning to their everyday world.

Weather and Seasons is divided into four chapters. Chapter one, "Weather and Seasonal Experiments," is designed to help children think logically and productively, especially about real, concrete things. The experiments have the following format:

Problem: The title poses a question that asks students to think, discuss, and hypothesize answers. Children may make predictions about ways to solve the problem.

Materials: A general list of supplies is provided for each activity. Adjust the quantities according to the number of children involved.

Preparation: This section lists steps taken by the adult before beginning the activity. Most activities call for active involvement on the part of the children. However, when an experiment is an adult demonstration because of safety considerations, this is indicated in the preparation section.

Activity: This section lists the steps in the activity. Children are encouraged to explore and discover.

Observations: Children are encouraged to sharpen their awareness of what they see or experience in the activity.

Variation: Variations are listed for certain experiments, often suggesting adaptations of the experiments for children who are able to read and write or do math computations.

Things to Wonder About: These questions and follow-up activities are designed to help children question the world around them and to extend what they've learned to their daily life.

In chapters two and three, "Science and the Curriculum" and "Science and the Creative Arts," weather and seasons is the organizing theme for language arts, math, social living, art, literature and movement. The focus in chapter two is on higher level thinking skills and creativity. Self-esteem is fostered through discussion, problem solving, and open-ended activities.

In chapter three, art activities emphasize the process, not the final product. The art activities are open-ended and will not be threatening to children who don't know how to draw. The creative movement activities encourage children to express themselves in a variety of creative ways. Chapters two and three have the following format:

Materials: A list of supplies is provided for each activity. Adjust according to the number of children doing the activity.

Preparation: This sections lists anything the adult needs to do before beginning the activity.

Activity: This lists the steps in the activity.

Variations: Variations are listed for certain activities, often suggesting adaptations for children who are able to read and write or do math computations.

The literature section is a resource list of related children's books for parents and teachers to read to children. Teachers should read children these selections during their story hour. Selections can be left in the classroom library or by the science center for children to look at or read.

Chapter One:

Weather & Seasonal Experiments

SUNNY DAYS

How does a thermometer work?

Materials: Outdoor thermometer, ice cubes, small container, rubber bands

Activity: Show the thermometer. Tell the children that the red line (the mercury) in the thermometer becomes long or short depending upon how warm it is. Put a rubber band around the temperature reading on the thermometer. Ask the children what they think will happen to the red line on the thermometer if it is put outside. Place the thermometer outside, and compare the difference in temperature after a while. Put another rubber band around the temperature reading. Ask the children what they think will happen to the red line on the thermometer when it is placed in ice cubes. Fill the small container with ice cubes, and put the thermometer in it for a few seconds.

Observations: Is the red line higher inside or outside? Is the red line higher or lower after we put it in ice cubes?

Variation: Older children can learn how to read and record the daily temperature.

Why do we wear light-colored clothing on a sunny day?

Materials: Black cloth, white cloth

Activity: Show the children a piece of black cloth and a similar cloth that is white. Ask the children which cloth they think will get hot faster: the black cloth or the white cloth. Place both pieces of cloth in a sunny spot for at least 15 minutes. Have the children touch each piece of cloth and compare the temperatures.

Observations: Which cloth feels warmer?

Things to Wonder About: Does white cloth always stay cooler than the other colors? Why do we wear colors such as white, light blue, light yellow, or beige on a summer day? Why do we wear colors such as black, navy, or brown on a winter day? What would happen if we set a dark brown cloth and a light blue cloth in the sun? Which would stay cooler?

What happens to milk left in the sun?

Materials: Milk, two clear plastic tumblers, marker

Activity: On a very hot day, fill two plastic tumblers with equal amounts of milk. Mark the milk levels. Place one tumbler in the hot sun and the other in the refrigerator. Ask the children what they think will happen. Have the children compare the differences between the milk left in the sun and the milk left in the refrigerator.

Observations: How does the milk that was in the sun look? Smell it. Do you think it would taste bad? Does this milk look and smell different from the milk left in the refrigerator?

Things to Wonder About: What other foods might curdle or spoil in the sun?

What happens to wet objects left in the sun?

Materials: Three containers, mud, paint, playdough

Activity: Place mud, paint, and playdough in the containers. Have the children close their eyes and use their senses of smell, touch, and hearing to try to identify the mud, paint, and playdough. Ask the children what they think would happen to the materials if the containers were left in the hot sun. Place the containers in the sun for a day, and then have the children observe the changes.

Observations: What do the mud, paint, and playdough look like after being in the sun? Which looks and feels the driest?

Things to Wonder About: Can you think of other wet things that the sun dries? What happens when you're wet and go outside on a sunny day? What would happen if we put the containers in the freezer? Which would get hard first?

WINDY DAYS

What can air move?

Materials: Hair dryer, objects of different weights (rock, paper, feather, cotton ball, shoe, block, balloon, paper clip)

Activity: Go on a treasure hunt for heavy and light objects. Have the children sort and classify all the objects as light or heavy. Turn on the hair dryer, and point it at different objects.

Observations: Which objects can the air from the hair dryer move? How are the objects alike? How are they different?

Things to Wonder About: What happens to papers when they are left outside on a windy day? Do rocks move when the wind blows?

Which things hold more air?

Materials: Balloon, paper bag, plastic bag

Activity: Fill the balloon, paper bag, and plastic bag with air. Have the children observe and feel each inflated object. Release the air. Have the children compare the differences between the inflated and deflated balloon, paper sack, and plastic bag. Fill them with air again, and ask the children which one they think will make the loudest noise when popped. Then pop the inflated objects.

Observations: What are the things like with air in them? What are they like when we let the air out?

Variation: Fill a basin with water. Blow up two balloons. Which noise will be louder: a balloon popped on the floor or a balloon popped underwater?

Things to Wonder About: How can you make your cheeks bigger? What else gets bigger when it's filled with air?

What does the wind do to wet objects?

Materials: Water, three paper towels, paper fan, hair dryer

Activity: Wet the paper towels. Ask the children to think of ways to make the paper towels dry. Then dry one towel outside in the wind, dry another with the wind of a paper fan, and dry the last with the wind of a hair dryer. Ask the children which they think will dry the fastest.

Observations: Which towel dried the fastest? Do the paper towels look different after they've dried? Use the senses of sight, touch, smell, and hearing to notice changes in the paper towels when wet and dry.

Things to Wonder About: Will clothes dry faster on a windy day than on a still one?

RAINY DAYS

Does water make something heavier?

Materials: Plastic shower-curtain liner, plastic jug, water, large bucket

Activity: Cover the work area with plastic. Have the children lift the empty jug. Fill the jug with water, and have the children lift it. Then have one of the children hold the bucket while you pour the water from the jug into the bucket.

Observations: Which is heavier: the empty jug or the one with water in it? Does the bucket feel heavier as it fills with water?

Things to Wonder About: How many jugs of water would it take to fill the bucket halfway? How many would it take to fill it to the top?

Which container holds the most water?

Materials: Water, plastic measuring cup, pint container, quart container, empty soda bottle, rose vase

Activity: Fill the measuring cup with water. Fill the pint container with water, using the measuring cup as a measure. Have the children count the number of cups it takes to fill the container. Then fill the other containers while the children count the number of cups it takes to fill each one.

Observations: Which container takes the most cups of water to fill? Is it the tallest?

Things to Wonder About: If you used quart containers with different shapes (plastic tub, soda bottle, milk container) which would hold the most water? How many pint containers of water does it take to fill the quart container? How many quart containers of water does it take to fill the gallon container?

Do things weigh the same when they are wet?

Materials: Pan balance scale, two measuring cups, sand, water

Activity: Put two empty measuring cups on each side of the pan balance scale. Put water in one measuring cup, and have the children observe which cup is heavier. Empty the cup of water. Then put dry sand in both cups and weigh them. Pour water in one cup of dry sand, and weigh the cups.

Observations: Which weighs more: the empty cup or the one with water? The cup with wet sand or dry sand? Does water make sand heavier? Does water make the sand look different?

Things to Wonder About: What would happen if you did the same experiment with cornmeal or sponges? Try it!

What kinds of paper will soak up water?

Materials: Water, waxed paper, paper towel, newspaper, construction paper, sandpaper, finger-painting paper, cup, eye dropper

Activity: Show the children the different types of paper. Have them name them. Ask the children to look at and feel the paper and then predict which ones they think are the best for soaking up water. Then put a drop of water in the middle of each paper.

Observations: Which papers soaked up water?

Things to Wonder About: What would happen if you heated the water? Would it soak into the paper faster than cold water? Use a timer to see if hot or cold water soaks into a newspaper faster.

What things dissolve in water?

Materials: Water, six clear plastic tumblers, teaspoons, salt, sugar, flour, cornstarch, sand, bread

Activity: Pour an equal amount of water in each plastic tumbler. Have the children close their eyes and smell, touch, taste, hear (when applicable), and then see the dry ingredients. Ask the children to predict what will happen when a teaspoon of salt is added to the tumbler of water. Put the salt in the tumbler, and stir it. After the children have observed what happens to the salt, repeat the experiment using sugar, flour, cornstarch, sand, and bread.

Observations: Did the salt disappear? How has the color changed? Did all of the other things disappear in water?

Things to Wonder About: What would happen to a glass jar filled with water if oil was added? Try it! Does the oil disappear when it's shaken? What happens to the oil after it stands for a while?

How can we make rain?

Materials: Teakettle, water, hot plate or stove, saucepan, ice

Preparation: This is an adult demonstration. Caution children to stay away from the steam.

Activity: Fill the teakettle with water, and heat it until the water boils. Discuss safety precautions when handling hot things. Fill the saucepan with ice. Place the saucepan above the steam from the teakettle. Talk about how the steam is like a cloud. When the warm steam hits the cold pan, "rain drops" form on the outside of the pan.

Observations: How is the bottom of the saucepan changing? Why did this happen?

Things to Wonder About: What do you see in the sky just before it rains? What do you think makes rain fall from the clouds?

What makes a rainbow?

Materials: Source of bright light, clear glass, piece of white paper

Activity: Partially fill the glass with water. Look for a bright beam of sunlight. Place the glass of water near the light beam. Place the white paper behind the glass. Discuss how the sunlight bends when it enters the water and leaves the water. This causes light to separate and make a rainbow. When the sun is brightly shining outside and it rains, the raindrops cause the sunlight to bend to form a rainbow.

Observations: What do you see on the white paper? Name the colors in the band. Note: There are seven colors in the rainbow—violet, indigo, blue, green, yellow, orange, and red.

Things to Wonder About: What do you see when you water grass with a lawn sprinkler or hose on a sunny day?

SNOWY DAYS

How can we make frost?

Materials: Tin can (without a label), crushed ice, rock salt, glass, water

Activity: Discuss places where the children have seen frost outside on a very cold day. Fill the tin can with a layer of crushed ice, then rock salt, then crushed ice, then rock salt. Let the can sit for a while. Then have the children observe how the water vapor has changed into ice crystals. Fill a glass with ice water, and have the children compare the can and the glass.

Observations: What do you see forming on the outside of the can? Compare the outside of the can with the glass of ice water. Does the glass have frost on the outside? How are the two containers alike? Different?

Things to Wonder About: What do you see when you breathe or talk outside on a very cold day?

How can we stay warm on a cold day?

Materials: Four coffee cans, pieces of fur, terry cloth, knit material, waxed paper, rubber bands, hot water

Activity: Wrap each bottle with fur, terry cloth, knit material, or waxed paper. Secure with rubber bands. Have the children feel and identify the fur, terry cloth, knit material, and waxed paper. Have the children predict which can will stay the warmest. Put the cans in sequential order according to the predictions. Fill each can with hot water and have the children feel them. After 20 minutes, have the children feel the cans again.

Observations: Which is the warmest? Which is the coldest?

Things to Wonder About: Why do you wear gloves on your hands on a cold day? On a cold day, feel a window with gloves. Then take them off and feel the window.

What will melt an ice cube?

Materials: Cold, warm, and hot water, ice cubes, three small pans

Activity: Have the children examine an ice cube. Talk about ways to make the ice cube melt. Put three ice cubes (all the same size) in three pans of cold, warm, and hot water. Discuss safety precautions when handling hot things. Have the children choose the pan they think will melt ice cube the fastest.

Observations: What happens when the ice cubes melt? Which one turned to water first?

Variation: Take one ice cube, wrap it in a plastic bag, and crush it with a hammer. Put it in a pan. Put a cube in another pan. Observe which ice will melt more quickly: crushed or cube. Time the melting process. Younger children can use a timer; older children can use a clock.

Things to Wonder About: What happens to icicles or frost on a sunny day?

What else will melt an ice cube?

Materials: Table salt, pepper, sugar, ice cubes, three small bowls, tablespoon

Activity: Have the children use their sense of touch, smell, taste, and sight to examine the table salt, sugar, and pepper. Put three ice cubes (all the same size) in three small bowls. Place a tablespoon of table salt on the first ice cube, a tablespoon of sugar on the second ice cube, and a tablespoon of pepper on the third ice cube.

Observations: Which ice cube melted first?

Things to Wonder About: Can you think of ways we can prevent people from falling on an icy sidewalk or driveway in winter? Why do freshwater lakes freeze faster than saltwater bodies of water?

Does the same amount of snow fall everywhere?

Materials: Three long sticks or yard sticks, three rubber bands

Activity: Go outside and have the children observe the snow on the ground. Pick three locations to measure the depth of the snow. Have children predict which location will have the most snow. Measure the snow with the long sticks. Mark each measurement with a rubber band.

Observations: Where was the snow the deepest?

Variation: Older children can measure the depth using yardsticks or they can bring the sticks indoors and measure with rulers and yardsticks.

Things to Wonder About: Why is there more snow against a building than there is in an open area?

Chapter Two:

Science & the Curriculum

LANGUAGE ARTS

Rain Changes Things

Materials: Paper, crayon or marker

Activity: Take the children for a walk on a rainy day or a have them look out the window. Observe the wet objects outside. Then brainstorm with the children. Have them think of all the words they can to describe the things they saw. Make a chart of the words they use. On a sunny day, have the children observe the same objects and describe them. Make a chart of the words the children use to describe the objects when they are dry. Compare the two charts, and discuss how rain changes thngs.

Variation: Older children can write down the words they think of to describe the objects when they are wet and when they are dry. Using the adjectives, children can pick an object and write an imaginary story about it on a rainy day.

Something to Touch

Materials: Box, scissors, adhesive shelf paper, "warm" objects (velvet, yarn, pot holder), "cold" objects (metal spoon, glass paperweight, ceramic tile), paper, crayon or marker.

Preparation: Cover the box with the shelf paper. Cut a round hole on the top of the box large enough for a hand to fit through. Put the objects in the box.

Activity: Have the children put their hands inside the box and describe what each article is made of and how it feels to the touch. Children can look around the class or house for other articles they can classify as warm or cold to the touch. Then place small metal articles and pieces of cloth in a sunny spot in the room and a duplicate set of articles in a cool spot. After a while, bring both sets of items together. Have the children close their eyes and feel the difference in temperature between the sets. Give the children paper, and let them draw a picture of a warm object on one side and a cool object on the other side. The children can dictate a sentence about their drawings.

Variation: Older children can pick a warm and cool object and write a story about the warm object in a warm climate and the cool object in a cold climate.

Seasonal Sounds

Materials: Magazines or catalogs, scissors, glue, oaktag, four sheets of construction paper, stapler

Preparation: Cut out pictures related to seasons or weather (mitten, scarf, Santa, tulip, kite, wind, boat, water, bunny, barbecue, leaf, witch, pumpkin). Mount the pictures on oaktag. Make four pocket envelopes by folding the sheets of construction paper in half and stapling two sides. Glue a seasonal picture on each pocket.

Activity: Have the children name the picture and tell the initial consonant sound. After the initial consonant sounds have been identified, have the children classify the season they would find these pictures. Put them in the appropriate seasonal envelopes.

Sequencing Seasons

Materials: Four small boxes, adhesive shelf paper or construction paper (white, pink, yellow, red), scissors, glue, magazines or catalogs

Preparation: Cover the boxes with shelf paper or construction paper. Make the winter box white, the spring box pink, the summer box yellow, and the fall box red. Paste a seasonal picture on each box, and label the box with its season. Cut out many seasonal pictures (ice, rain, sun, leaves, evergreens, crocuses, roses, mums, ice-skating, Christmas trees, Easter eggs, fireworks, jack-o'-lanterns, wool hats, jackets, bathing suits).

Activity: Have the children look at all the pictures and name them. Show the children the seasonal boxes and have them name the seasons and put the boxes in sequential order. Have the children match the pictures and place them with their appropriate seasonal boxes. (Some pictures could be placed in more than one box.)

Variation: For older children, print seasonal words on index cards. Have the children read all the words and put them in order according to their seasons.

Animal Homes

Materials: Magazines or catalogs, scissors, glue, oaktag or construction paper

Preparation: Cut out pictures of animals and animal homes (dog/doghouse, horse/barn, bear/cave, beaver/beaver lodge, fish/river, frog/lily pond, squirrel/tree). Mount them on oaktag or on construction paper.

Activity: Discuss the different types of animal homes. Talk about how some animals build their own homes, some find homes, and some live in homes people build for them. Talk about how animals survive in the winter, discussing how some hibernate and others move to warmer places.

Have the children match the animals with their homes. Group the animal homes according to whether they are made by the animals, "found" homes, or made by people.

MATH

Sorting Boots and Sandals

Materials: Boots in winter, sandals in summer

Preparation: In winter, collect boots the children have worn to school. Place the boots in the middle of the floor. (Do the same with sandals on a summer day.)

Activity: Have the children sort the shoes in various ways: by color, by size, by material, by style, or by left and right. Compare the number of shoes in each set.

Variation: Older children can do addition problems by adding two sets and finding a sum.

Measuring Months

Materials: Lunch bags, seasonal objects

Preparation: Each season, take a nature walk with the children, and collect seasonal objects (no larger than a child's thumb) in lunch bags.

Activity: Have the children identify, compare, count, and measure the contents of their bags. Make a seasonal graph of the objects, listing the types of objects found each season and showing how some objects change from one season to another.

Counting Weather

Materials: Calendar, scissors, tinsel, yellow construction paper, white tissue paper, cotton balls, glue

Preparation: Cut the tinsel into small pieces. Cut yellow circles from the construction paper. Cut small squares of white tissue paper.

Activity: Each day of the month observe the weather. When it's a cloudy day, paste the tissue paper on that day on the calendar. When it's a sunny day, paste on a yellow circle. When it's a rainy day, paste on tinsel. When it's a snowy day, paste on a cotton ball. At the end of the month, have the children count all the sunny, snowy, cloudy, and rainy days. Have the children compare the number of days for each type of weather.

Variation: Older children can add the number of rainy days and find the sum. They can subtract the number of rainy days from the total days in the month and find the difference.

Partnering Pairs

Materials: Pairs of various seasonal items (mittens, swim goggles, boots, knee socks, ankle socks, sandals, ice skates, swim flippers, tennis shoes, soccer shoes, ear muffs, furry slippers, sneakers)

Preparation: Put pairs of various objects in a pile on the floor.

Activity: Have the children name all the objects. Identify the season in which these objects would be worn. Discuss the meaning of the word "pair." Have the children sort through the pile and classify all the pairs.

Variation: Older children can practice writing the numeral 2. Have them practice writing it in flour, sand, or salt before using pencil and paper.

Mercury Magic

Materials: Large outdoor thermometer, scissors, red yarn, paper, glue

Activity: Show the children the thermometer and discuss how a thermometer works. Then put it in a cool spot. After a while, have the children look at the mercury. Let them measure the length of the mercury by cutting a piece of red yarn the same length as the mercury in the thermometer. Paste the yarn on a piece of paper. Put the thermometer in a warm spot. After a while, have the children look at the mercury and measure it by cutting another piece of yarn. Paste the yarn on the paper next to the yarn that represents the cooler temperature. Have the children compare the length of the pieces of yarn. Repeat the activity on different days, using different locations. Make a chart using the yarn lengths.

Variation: Older children can learn the symbols for greater than (〉) and less than (〈).

Making Up Patterns

Materials: Pinecones in winter, umbrellas in spring, seashells or rocks in summer, and leaves in autumn

Preparation: Collect pinecones in winter months, seashells or rocks in summer months, and leaves in autumn. In spring, collect the children's umbrellas.

Activity: Have the children sort their collections each season. For example, in fall help the children look at leaves in terms of color, shape, and type (flat, curled, simple). Have them sort umbrellas by color, size, length of handle, design, and material. Have the children then create repeating patterns from their collections. For example, a pattern of umbrellas might be plastic/cloth/plastic/cloth; a pattern of leaves might be yellow/brown/red/yellow/brown/red.

I Feel Heavy

Materials: Paper, marker, scale, winter coats, hats, boots, mittens, scarves, sweaters

Preparation: Make a chart with three columns. List the children's names on the left-hand side. Draw a picture of a child without a coat above the next column and a child with a coat above the last column.

Activity: Weigh the children when they have their outdoor clothes on, and record their weights. Weigh them again after they have removed their outdoor clothes, and record their weights. Compare the different weights, and discuss how heavy the children feel when they are dressed for very cold weather.

Basket of Leaves

Materials: Fall leaves, rake, rectangular laundry basket and round laundry basket of equal weight and capacity, scale

Preparation: Take the children outside and have them rake leaves into piles. Fill both laundry baskets with leaves. Have the children predict which basket will weigh more. Then weigh both laundry baskets full of leaves and compare their weights. Discuss the predictions and the results.

SOCIAL LIVING

Seasonal Workers

Materials: Magazines or catalogs, scissors, glue, oaktag or construction paper

Preparation: Cut out pictures of seasonal workers (lifeguards, ice cream truck drivers, baseball players, football players, hockey players, basketball players, snowplow operators, skiers, furnace service people). Mount the pictures on oaktag or construction paper.

Activity: Show pictures of these workers and have the children identify them and the jobs they perform. Discuss how weather effects their jobs: How do their jobs change when weather and seasons change? Which workers are busy on snowy days? Sunny days? All seasons? Have the children decide which people are busy in the summer but not in the winter.

Weather and Homes

Materials: Magazines or catalogs, scissors, glue, oaktag or construction paper, index cards

Preparation: Cut out pictures of various homes, such as an apartment, single-family home, tent, trailer, bungalow, beach house, camper, and ski lodge. Mount them on oaktag or construction paper. Cut out a scene for winter, spring, summer, and fall, and glue the pictures on index cards.

Activity: Have the children name each home. Then have the children identify the seasonal scenes. Discuss how some homes and buildings are built for specific weather or seasons. Ask the children to pick homes that would be best for each season, and have them discuss the reasons why.

Variation: With older children, write winter, spring, summer, and fall on the index cards.

Water Watchers

Materials: Magazines or catalogs, scissors, glue, oaktag or construction paper, paper, crayon or marker

Preparation: Cut out pictures of ways we use water (washing cars, bathing, faucets, brushing teeth, washing dishes, washing vegetables, watering lawns). Mount the pictures on oaktag or construction paper.

Activity: Discuss ways we use water. Talk about what our lives woud be like without water, asking the children to think of things they wouldn't have or couldn't do if we didn't have water. Brainstorm about ways we waste water and ways we can save water. Record the answers on an experience chart.

Seasonal Transportation

Materials: Magazines or catalogs, scissors, glue, oaktag or construction paper

Preparation: Cut out pictures of seasonal transportation (snowplows, sleds, skis, snow shoes, row boats, sailboats, campers, convertibles, hot-air balloons, trucks, motorcycles, bicycles, tricycles, skateboards, roller skates, horses). Mount the pictures on oaktag or construction paper.

Activity: Discuss the word "transportation." Show the pictures of different ways of traveling and have the children identify them. Ask the children what type of weather is best for each vehicle. Ask them what would happen if we traveled on a sled on a sunny day or in a convertible on a rainy day? Then have the children pick one way of traveling and take an imaginary trip on a snowy, rainy, sunny, or windy day.

Variation: With older children, word cards can be substituted for pictures. Have the children alphabetize the words, and then discuss the vehicles and match them with the weather.

Chapter Three:

Science & the Creative Arts

ART

Seasonal Tree

Materials: Large tree branch, large metal can, plaster of paris or clay

Preparation: Place the tree branch in the metal can. Secure it by filling the can with clay or plaster of paris.

Activity: Discuss the four seasons. Discuss characteristics of each season. Take a nature walk, and collect outdoor items for the indoor tree. In fall, collect and attach fall leaves and acorns to the tree. Place apples on the tree and ground. In winter, attach pine needles and pinecones. In spring, find forsythia or cherry blossoms. (If natural products aren't available, make forsythia or cherry blossoms by crumpling tissue paper and gluing it on the tree). Have the children find or make nests. In summer, collect green leaves.

Variation: The season tree can also be decorated for different holidays.

Ice Cube Painting

Materials: Finger-painting paper, finger paints, spoon, ice cubes (freeze Popsicle sticks in cubes for easy handling), skating music such as the "Skater's Waltz"

Preparation: Put finger paint on the paper with a spoon. Give each child an ice cube.

Activity: Have the children create a picture, using the ice cube instead of a brush, while listening to the music.

Variation: Use snow instead of ice.

My Furry Mittens

Materials: Scissors, oaktag, pencil, glue, yarn, fur scraps, hole punch

Preparation: Cut oaktag into small squares the size of a child's hand.

Activity: Have the children trace on the oaktag the outline of their left thumb and remaining four fingers in the shape of a mitten. Do the same with the right hand. Have the children cut out the mittens and decorate them with yarn and fur scraps. Punch holes at the bottom corners of the mittens and fasten them together with yarn.

Soapy Snow People

Materials: Soap flakes, mixing bowl, hand or electric mixer, water, Popsicle sticks or twigs, tiny pebbles, yarn, ribbon, fabric scraps

Preparation: Pour soap flakes into the bowl. Add a small amount of water to the soap flakes. Whip with mixer until the mixture is of a consistency that can be formed into a ball. Discuss the fact that we should never eat soap because it will make us sick.

Activity: Have the children form a large ball for the body and small ball for the head. Decorate the snow person with a pebble face, sticks or twigs for arms, and yarn, ribbon, or fabric scraps for a scarf.

Snow Scenes

Materials: Large washable table, shaving cream, small toy cars and trucks, toy animals and people, washable odds and ends, leaves, twigs, rocks, pinecones

Preparation: Spray shaving cream on the table.

Activity: Have the children create winter scenes. Provide props such as empty margarine containers, toy animals and people, pine tree twigs, sticks, toy cars and trucks, and cans.

Variation: In the summer months, add blue food coloring and create an ocean of blue waves. Add props for a swim scenario!

Raining Tinsel

Materials: White construction paper, markers, water-based paint, paint brush, water, tinsel, glue

Activity: Have the children draw a bridge shape on the white construction paper. The children then use the shape to create an umbrella or a picture showing a rainy day. Have them paint the ground and sky. When the paint dries, have the children glue on tinsel to represent rain.

Sprinkling Rain

Materials: Salt shakers with very small holes, sand, powdered tempera paints, paste, finger-paint paper, "The Water Music Suite" by Handel

Preparation: Fill each salt shaker with powdered paint. Secure the lids tightly. Wet the paper.

Activity: While listening to classical music, have the children shake "rain" on the wet finger-paint paper.

Variation: Have the children put powdered tempera on the paper. Don't wet the paper. Go outside and let the rain wet the paper.

Fog Picture

Materials: Construction paper, scissors, markers or crayons, magazines, glue, white tissue paper, tape

Preparation: Cut the tissue paper so that it's the same size as the construction paper.

Activity: Have the children draw an outdoor picture with markers or crayons. Or have them cut and paste outdoor pictures from magazines. Cover the picture with a piece of white tissue paper. Tape the tissue paper to the construction paper at the top. Have the children "lift the fog" and uncover their outdoor scenes.

Cloud Differences

Materials: Blue construction paper, white cotton balls, gray and white feathers, lint from clothes dryer, glue

Preparation: Have the children go outside and observe the clouds, looking at their color and shapes. Explain that cumulus clouds are white, fluffy clouds. Cirrus clouds are the fast-moving, thin, white clouds. Stratus clouds are thin, grayish white clouds that cover most of the sky in streaks. Nimbus clouds are dark gray rain clouds.

Activity: Have the children glue cotton balls, feathers, or lint on blue construction paper in the shape of the clouds they observe.

Wave Painting

Materials: Blue construction paper, glue, sand, white paint, sponge, shells, crayons or markers

Activity: Have the children create a beach scene. Glue sand on the blue construction paper. Make waves by using the sponge and the white paint. When the sand and paint are dry, have the children draw people and fish, and glue on shells for the beach scene.

Wind Painting

Materials: Construction paper, spoon, powdered tempera paint (red, yellow, blue), straws

Activity: Spoon red, yellow, and blue paint on the construction paper. Have the children blow through straws and feel their own wind. Have them try to use their wind to move the paint by blowing through the straws.

Variation: Try the activity outside on a slightly windy day, letting the wind move the paint.

CREATIVE MOVEMENT

Snow Walks

Activity: Have the children pretend they wake up, look out the window, and see snow falling softly to the ground. Ask them to create movements to show how they would move: How do you walk with boots and heavy coats on? How would you drive a car? How would you move on skates? How would you move on a sled quickly going down a hill? How would you move on a snowplow?

Pull the Sled

Activity: Have the children work with partners. One child will pull the sled; the other will be the sled in the snow. The "sled" puts his or her hands on the puller's waist to represent a rope. The puller drags the sled through the snow until they come to a hill. They have trouble getting up the hill. When they reach the top of the hill, the puller moves behind the sled, and the sled runs quickly down the hill.

Dry Me

Activity: Have the children move their bodies as if they were soaking wet pieces of fabric. Have them move their heads, torsos, legs, and feet as if they were filled with water. Then ask them to try to get the water out of the fabric. Let the children show you how they would do this, moving their bodies as if they were being wrung and squeezed, shaken, or pounded. Ask them if they felt heavier when they were wet or when they were dry.

Muddy Movements

Activity: Have the children pretend they're moving in mud. They feel gooey, sticky, and heavy. Allow the children to move freely around to dramatize walking in mud. Tell them the mud is beginning to freeze and have them slow their movements until they're frozen in one position. Then tell them the sun has come out, and the mud is slowly thawing. They can move a bit at a time, until they move through the mud and jump out!

Water Washes Things

Activity: Dramatize washing clothes in a washing machine. Have the children hold their arms out horizontally to represent a washing machine: The machine is turned on and fills up with water. (The children are in a squatting position and slowly rise to a standing position.) Now the machine washes your clothes. (They twist back and forth). Your clothes need to be rinsed. (The children move from a standing position slowly to the floor. They then sit on their knees and hit the floor loudly to represent water rinsing and gushing.) Now the machine spins the water out of your clothes. (The children spin around in a circle). Finally, the clothes are clean. (Have the children quietly stop moving and rest). Discuss the difference between washing clothes in a stream and washing clothes in a washing machine.

Clothesline

Activity: Have a few children stand in a line holding hands to form the clothesline. A few more of the children pretend to be clothes. They stand between two people on the clothesline, touching their arms. Warm air is drying the clothes. The "clothes" move back and forth and under the clothesline. The children that are the clothesline shake their arms in the wind. As the wind picks up, so does the motion. When the clothes are dry, they are taken off the line. (Have the children sit down.) The clothes are then folded. (Have the children sit cross-legged, with their heads in their laps.)

Balloons

Activity: Have the children kneel on the floor. Tell them they are balloons and someone is filling them with air. The children slowly rise to a standing position. When the balloons are fully inflated, the children stand straight with their arms extended in circles over their heads. Have them sway back and forth like balloons moving in the wind. Then the air begins to escape, and they quickly drop their arms and sink back down to their knees.

Variation: Have the children find a partner. Supply a balloon for each pair. Ask: How many body parts can you use to tap your balloon to your partner? Can you hop while tapping your balloon? Tap the balloon using right hand, left hand, and both hands, alternating with palm and back of hand. Using your balloon, play catch with your partner. Tap the balloon back and forth.

Kiddie Kites

Materials: Yarn

Preparation: Have the children work with partners. Each of the partners holds one end of the yarn.

Activity: One child is the kite. The child with the other end of the yarn is the person flying a kite on a windy day. The kite lies down. The kite-owner wraps the yarn into a ball. The children pretend it's a windy day. The kite rises while the owner releases some of the string. The wind picks up and begins blowing very fiercely. The kite-owner unwraps more yarn. The kite runs, swings, sways, and twists as if he or she were a real kite blowing wildly in the wind.

LITERATURE

SUNNY DAYS

Berenstain, Stan and Jan. *The Berenstain Bears Go to Camp.* Random House, New York, 1982.

De Paola, Tomie. *The Quicksand Book.* Holiday House, New York, 1984.

McCloskey, Robert. *The Time of Wonder.* Viking Press, New York, 1957.

Zion, Gene. *Summer Snowman.* Harper & Row, New York, 1955.

Zolotow, Charlotte. *Summer Is.* Thomas Y. Crowell, New York, 1983.

WINDY DAYS

Berenstain, Stan and Jan. *The Berenstain Bears Go Fly a Kite.* Random House, New York, 1983.

Ets, Marie Hall. *Gilberto and the Wind.* Viking Press, New York, 1963.

Greene, Carol. *Please, Wind?* Children's Press, Chicago, 1982.

Hutchins, Pat. *The Wind Blew.* Macmillan, New York, 1974.

Keats, Ezra Jack. *Whistle for Willie.* Viking Press, New York, 1964.

Lamorisse, Albert. *The Red Balloon.* Doubleday, New York, 1957.

Rey, Margaret. *Curious George Flies a Kite.* Houghton Mifflin, Boston, 1958.

Zolotow, Charlotte. *When the Wind Stops.* Harper & Row, New York, 1975.

RAINY DAYS

Barret, Judi. *Cloudy with a Chance of Meatballs.* Atheneum, New York, 1978.

Branley, Franklyn. *Flash, Crash, Rumble, and Roll.* Thomas Y. Crowell, New York, 1983.

_____. *Rain and Hail.* Thomas Y. Crowell, New York, 1983.

Brewer, Mary. *What Floats?* Children's Press, Chicago, 1976.

Burningham, John. *Mr. Gumpy's Motor Car.* Thomas Y. Crowell, New York, 1973.

De Paola, Tomie. *The Cloud Book.* Holiday House, New York, 1975.

Greene, Carol. *Rain! Rain!* Children's Press, Chicago, 1982.

_____. *Hi Clouds.* Children's Press, Chicago, 1983.

Hall, Adelaide. *The Rain Puddle.* Lothrop, Lee, & Shepard, New York, 1965.

Kalan, Robert. *Rain.* Greenwillow, New York, 1978.

Renberg, Dalia Hardof. *Hello Clouds!* Harper & Row, New York, 1985.

Shaw, Charles G. *It Looked Like Spilt Milk.* Harper & Row, New York, 1947.

Skofield, James. *All Wet! All Wet!* Harper & Row, New York, 1984.

Spiers, Peter. *Rain.* Doubleday, New York, 1982.

Szilagyi, Mary. *The Thunderstorm Book.* Bradbury Press, New York, 1985.

Tresselt, Alvin. *Hide and Seek Fog.* Lothrop, Lee, & Shepard, New York, 1965.

Zolotow, Charlotte. *The Storm Book.* Harper & Row, New York, 1952.

SNOWY DAYS

Bedford, Annie North. *Frosty the Snowman.* Western, Racine, WI, 1950.

Branley, Franklyn. *Snow Is Falling.* Thomas Y. Crowell, New York, 1961.

Brenner, Barbara. *The Penguin Who Hated the Cold.* Random House, New York, 1973.

Burton, Virginia Lee. *Katy and the Big Snow.* Houghton Mifflin, Boston, 1974.

Greene, Carol. *Ice Is . . . Whee!* Children's Press, New York, 1962.

Keats, Ezra Jack. *The Snowy Day.* Viking Press, New York, 1962.

Paterson, Diane. *The Biggest Snowstorm Ever.* Dial, New York, 1978.

Rey, Margaret and H.A. *Curious George Goes Sledding.* Houghton Mifflin, Boston, 1984.

Tresselt, Alvin. *The Mitten.* Lothrop, Lee, & Shepard, New York, 1964.

ABOUT THE AUTHOR

Lynn Cohen received her B.S. in education from S.U.N.Y. at New Paltz and M.S. in remedial reading from Johns Hopkins University. She is currently pursuing doctoral studies in early childhood education. She teaches early childhood and elementary education at S.U.N.Y. College at Old Westbury and kindergarten for the East Williston School District in New York. She also conducts in-service workshops for early childhood teachers. She has authored three other books, *Me and My World, Exploring My World,* and *Fairy Tale World* and has contributed articles for *Pre-K Today.*